Look- Alikes

Story by Janie Spaht Gill, Ph.D.
Illustrations by Bob Reese

DOMINIE PRESS
Pearson Learning Group

Outside the pet store,
Johnny looked about...

As people walked in, and
with their dogs, came out.

3

Mrs. Pout walked in, and when she came out...

She had a Pekinese dog with her same snout.

Mr. Near walked in, and when he appeared...

He had a schnauzer with his same beard.

Mr. Down came out,
and Johnny found...

His expression was
like his basset hound.

Mr. Blaine and his sheepdog looked the same.

Both bodies were covered with hair and mane.

Mrs. Lear walked in, and when she appeared...

Her cocker spaniel and she had similar ears.

When Mrs. Strudel walked out,
she looked like her poodle.

Their curly coats looked
just like little noodles.

The last to exit was Mr. Small.

He didn't look like his dog at all.

He walked toward Johnny
with a great big grin.

He said, "I saw you
when I went in."

"I knew right away
what I should do.
Here, Johnny, this dog
was meant for you!"

- Have the children draw a picture of a pet or stuffed animal. Then help them place the animals in categories: dogs, cats, birds, fish, bears, etc. Count the number of children who have something in each category. Create a bar graph with the results.

- Help the children develop oral language by having them identify things involved in pet care. List these things on a chart and have them illustrate each activity.

- Have the children identify other animals that can be found in a pet store. Write these animal names on the board and have each child illustrate one of the animals. On a bulletin board, draw an outline of a pet store. Have the children glue or staple their pets in the store. The title of this project could be *Our Pet Store*.

- Take the children on a field trip to a local pet store, or have a veterinarian come in and talk to the class about proper pet care.

About the Author

Dr. Janie Spaht Gill brings twenty-five years of teaching experience to her books for young children. During her career thus far, she has taught at every grade level, from kindergarten through college. Gill has a Ph.D. in reading education, with a minor in creative writing. She is currently residing in Lafayette, Louisiana with her husband, Richard. Her fresh, humorous topics are inspired by the things her students say in the classroom. Gill was voted the 1999-2000 Louisiana Elementary Teacher of the Year for her outstanding work in primary education.

To my granddaughter
Lanie
From Janie

Softcover Edition ISBN 0-7685-2161-0
Library Bound Edition ISBN 0-7685-2469-5

Printed in Singapore
          12 13 14 VOZF 14 13 12 11

**Dominie
Press**

Pearson Learning Group

**1-800-321-3106
www.pearsonlearning.com**